Bringing Business Partnership to Life

The Story of the Brunei Window Washer

Praise for "Bringing Business Partnership to Life: The Story of the Brunei Window Washer"

"This entertaining offering from the Kirkpatricks clearly demonstrates how the effectiveness of a well-designed training program, tied to company values and expectations, transformed the life of a window washer and produced exceptional levels of engagement and business results. It is truly a model for all learning professionals to take heed and learn from in the ongoing challenge to demonstrate the value of training in any company."

Steve Ball
Manager, Learning and Development, Vale, Canada

"This is a compelling story based on a real life encounter that illustrates how training can demonstrably contribute to organizational excellence and personal success when it is designed and executed with the Kirkpatrick Foundational Principles in mind."

Andrew McK. Jefferson
CEO, Fort Hill Company

"Three years ago we decided to apply the Kirkpatrick evaluation methodology to each of our learning solutions, as relevant. It has been instrumental in helping us put numbers to the value we create and in demonstrating this clearly to the business. Now, with Jim's direct help, we have begun to take this to the next level."

Chris Jephson
Maersk Line

"This is a very user-friendly way to introduce the key concepts in the Kirkpatrick model. Jim's real experience is something we can all relate to, and this makes the model very easy to understand and implement in our own settings. I highly recommend this book for anyone who wants to make training more meaningful and partner effectively with management."

Barbara Carnes, Ph.D.
Co-Author of *Making Training Stick*

"By sharing an endearing tale of a window washer from Brunei, Jim and Wendy Kirkpatrick make the case for real life applications of 'The New World Kirkpatrick Model' and its usefulness as a return on investment strategy for learning organizations."

Dr. Marie A. Westbrook
Dean, College of Leadership Development,
Securities and Exchange Commission

"I encourage all learning professionals to read this book and apply the concepts. I have had the opportunity to hear Jim Kirkpatrick tell the story of the Brunei Window Washer and love the simple message. In their new book, Jim and Wendy Kirkpatrick demonstrate how critical it is for training professionals to form business partnerships before, during and after a learning event. These relationships, along with clearly established expectations, will help ensure that our training participants deliver the outcomes that our business leaders demand."

Jerry Brannen
Senior Learning Professional

"Jim and Wendy have certainly taken their work to the next level in this simple yet compelling tale that contains insightful truths. If every manager/supervisor understood the connection between training, job performance and worthwhile work, our employees could perform at much higher levels. The Kirkpatrick Business Partnership Model has the potential to transform learning and performance in our workplace today! This is a must read for every learning professional and manager."

Linda Hainlen
Director of Learning Solutions,
Indiana University Health

Other books by the Kirkpatricks

James D. and Wendy Kayser Kirkpatrick

Kirkpatrick Then and Now

Training on Trial

Donald L. and James D. Kirkpatrick

Evaluating Training Programs: The Four Levels

Implementing the Four Levels

Transferring Learning to Behavior

Donald L. Kirkpatrick

Improving Employee Performance Through Appraisal and Coaching

Developing Supervisors and Team Leaders

How to Conduct Productive Meetings

Managing Change Effectively

Bringing Business Partnership to Life

The Story of the Brunei Window Washer

JAMES D. KIRKPATRICK, PH.D.
WENDY KAYSER KIRKPATRICK

PRINTING HISTORY

This book was originally published under the title "The Brunei Window Washer: Bringing Business Partnership to Life" - April 2012

Kirkpatrick Partners
(443) 856-4500
information@kirkpatrickpartners.com
kirkpatrickpartners.com

The following marks are trademarks of Kirkpatrick Partners, LLC for use in education and training products, programs, services and books:
Kirkpatrick®
The One and Only Kirkpatrick®
Kirkpatrick Four Levels™

ISBN 1491032871
ISBN 13: 9781491032879

To all employees seeking to add value to their jobs, their companies and the world.

To all managers and supervisors tasked with developing the careers of their direct reports.

And most of all, to the many "Chais" of the world who largely go unrecognized.

Contents

PART III – Getting Started

Acknowledgements

This book would not have been possible without the generous support of many who helped to bring the characters and story to life. These people include Elaine Biech, Barbara Carnes, Linda Hainlen, Andy Jefferson, Martin Lowery, Mark Morrow, Ann Herrmann-Nehdi, Signe Schack Noesgaard and Marie Westbrook.

Thanks also to those who reviewed early manuscripts, including Steve Ball, Jerry Brannen, Lorri Freifeld, Chris Jephson and Bev Kaye.

Additional appreciation goes to those who worked their magic with the manuscript and illustrations, including Aestron Diniz, Mark Morrow, Barbie Kuntemeier, Lisa Schulteis, Allie Wehrman and Joy Wolf.

Finally, thanks to Don Kirkpatrick, Dad and Father-in-Law, for the inspiration behind everything we do.

Part I: The
Story of Chai

"Use what talents you possess, for
the woods would be a very silent
place if no birds sang there except
those birds that sang best."

Henry Van Dyke
U.S. author, educator and
clergyman

This book is based on a true story. Chai and the Unknown Window Washer (Benji) are real people. The initial interactions between the window washers and Dr. Jim Kirkpatrick are described just as they occurred.

From there, the story has been developed to show the likely outcomes for the two young men.

Enjoy the story!

Chapter 1
A Chance Meeting

May 2011
Grand Palace Hotel, Brunei

CHAI, A SLIM, cheerful-looking young man, approached the magnificent entrance of the Grand Palace Hotel in Brunei. *I can't believe I am entering the place where our country's highest dignitaries meet with the most important world leaders,* he thought.

Chai walked with a determined gait but hesitated for a moment before stepping onto the padded entrance carpet. As a resort employee at a different property, he had seldom entered through the beautiful and welcoming main entrance. He took a deep breath to consider what lay before him. *In just a few hours,* he thought, *I will be standing proud with all of the Premier Resort team members that have been promoted this year. I cannot believe that just over a year ago I was only a window washer.* And then, despite his best efforts to suppress it, a broad grin spread across his face.

Chai glanced quickly around the busy lobby. No one seemed to have noticed his daydreaming. He took this as a blessing and stepped onto the long red entrance carpet. Out of the corner of his eye, he noticed a man just about his age cleaning a large plate glass window by the entrance. He stopped again, this time to watch the window washer plunge a squeegee into a pail of hot, soapy water before lifting the dripping tool to the window. Chai smiled again and walked toward his fellow window washer.

"Hey, nice job you're doing," he called from a short distance. The window washer barely acknowledged him, offering only a slight, distracted nod before returning to his work. Chai was surprised by the fellow window washer's reaction; perhaps he hadn't heard him. Chai tried again, "I, too, have washed many windows." Again, little response. *So be it*, he thought. *Nothing can ruin this wonderful day.* He turned and entered the regal palace.

Chai glanced at his watch and saw that he had 30 minutes before meeting with his supervisor, Ms. Li. Despite his instinct to do something useful, he decided to take advantage of his unfamiliar status as a guest and relax in a comfortable, overstuffed chair near a sun-filled window.

Comfortably seated, Chai selected a newspaper from the array fanned out on the coffee table in front of him.

He had only flipped through a few pages when the thud of a rubber squeegee hitting the window caught his attention. The young man glanced in the direction of the sound. His eyes met the dull, expressionless stare of the unhappy window washer he had tried to engage in conversation a few moments earlier.

Chai lowered the newspaper to his lap and turned slightly to study the window washer at work. *Why is there no joy in his eyes,* he wondered. To Chai, each clean window was beautiful in its own right, something that instilled pride and accomplishment. *After all,* he thought happily, *washing windows is what gave me the good fortune to be here today!*

Chapter 2
A Memorable First Day

August 2009
The Premier Resort, Brunei

CHAI WAS EXCITED and nervous to be reporting for his first day of work at the Premier Resort, one of the most beautiful properties in all of Brunei. He had ridden his bicycle past the impressive resort on his way to school as a child. Entering the property for the first time seemed a symbolic beginning of a new chapter of his life.

Chai was reporting to work that day to begin his new position as a window washer. Although he was told by Ms. Anati, the Human Resources Manager, that the job was a first step in his career, he was just planning to do whatever the job required. He fully expected to be handed a bucket of water and a squeegee and told to get started.

The reality of the job did not worry Chai; for him, the

path was clear. He knew he was smart. He knew how to use a sponge and squeegee. And he knew one other thing: he intended to be the best window washer the resort had ever seen.

Perhaps that's why he was so surprised – shocked, really – when he and the other new employees were escorted into an elegant conference room overlooking the resort's beautifully landscaped golf course. When three crisply dressed catering associates entered the room, he was sure there had been some mistake. They carried a breakfast feast on silver trays that included fresh pastries, fruit, yogurt, coffee and juice. Chai was nothing short of speechless.

As the trio of servers arranged their trays along the center of the gleaming mahogany conference table, a well-dressed man who had been standing patiently near a bank of windows stepped forward. He smiled and thanked each of the servers by name before they left the room. The man waved his hand in the direction of the conference table and said, "Please, have some breakfast," in a cheerful, sincere voice. "This is all for you." As the new workers stood up and reached with some reluctance for the plates, the man introduced himself.

"Good morning. My name is Mr. Safrina, and I am the general manager of the Premier Resort." He continued, "I am here this morning to personally welcome you to our team and to tell you just how important your jobs are to me, the other employees of this resort, and especially our guests. You are joining a team that creates a great experience for every guest of the Premier Resort."

"Every job at the resort is of equal importance in meeting our highest goal, which is the sustained profitability of the resort," Mr. Safrina continued.

"You might wonder, as a member of the grounds keeping or catering staff, what impact you can have on profitability. I'll tell you. We track three key areas at the Premier Resort: team performance, guest experience and overall resort performance. You will see updated statistics each week on a poster like this in the employee break area." Mr. Safrina held up an example.

"I am not going to go into each measurement in detail, as they are broken down in various ways. Your supervisor will explain your exact responsibilities, how they will be tracked and reported, and how they contribute to our highest goal of a great experience for every guest."

"Every action you take and every customer you encounter here at the resort is an opportunity to increase guest satisfaction. When you do this, you increase the likelihood that guests will return to our resort and send their family and friends. This increases our occupancy and income. It also helps us to win awards, which also doesn't hurt in terms of being able to charge room rates that maintain our profitability," Mr. Safrina continued.

"I look at this poster, or dashboard as we call it, as a

The Premier Resort
Where we create a great experience for every guest!

Service Division - Monthly Performance Dashboard

	November 2009		
	Score	Target	Status
Team Performance Measures			
Daily shift meetings held	94%	95%	⇧
Weekly coaching sessions held	85%	95%	⇩
Weekly peer meetings held	80%	90%	⇨
Key responsibilities			
Core task completion score	91%	95%	⇩
Guest interaction score	92%	90%	⇧
Guest Experience Score			
Guest rooms	84%	90%	⇩
Grounds and facilities	89%	95%	⇧
Food service	95%	95%	⇨
Friendliness	96%	95%	⇧
Responsiveness	81%	90%	⬇
Overall satisfaction	88%	92%	⇨
Resort Performance			
Occupancy	–	–	⇧
Repeat guests	40%	40%	⇩
Industry excellence	3	2	⇧
Revenue	–	–	⇨
Overall Resort Performance	–	–	⇨

Compared to target

Green - at or above
Yellow - somewhat below
Red - significantly below

Compared to last month

⇧ - better
⇨ - same
⇩ - worse

Fig. 1 - The Premier Resort Service Team Dashboard

weekly picture of how well we are pleasing our guests and making this the best and most successful resort in all of Asia," Mr. Safrina said. "Notice the color-coding for each item: green for things that are going well, yellow for those not so good, and red for those areas that need immediate attention."

"Of course we want you to look forward to seeing the green items each week and celebrating your success," Mr. Safrina said with sincerity. "You may even see me visit your team meeting to pat you all on the back. But when yellows and especially reds appear, I and others on the senior leadership team will work with your managers to create a plan for all of us to turn the reds to yellows, and yellows to greens."

"All of this starts with training," Mr. Safrina said. "As you go through your training, I encourage you to view each new task you learn through the eyes of our guests. When they see beautifully maintained gardens, how does it make them feel? Or when they eat a delicious meal, note the crispness of the sheets, or get a nice smile from one of you? Each and every one of these actions helps all of us to be successful."

Mr. Safrina continued his explanation of the privilege and responsibility of taking care of all of the resort guests. As he spoke the words, "your job is just as important as mine," Chai felt that Mr. Safrina was speaking directly to *him*.

Interestingly, it was the same message Chai had gotten

from Ms. Anati, who had hired him a few weeks earlier. "Whether you cook, clean, or wash the windows, you are part of a larger team that is responsible for creating great experiences for our guests," she had told Chai. "Your face-to-face interaction is what really brings the spirit of the resort, and Brunei, to life for them."

Chai listened with great interest as Mr. Safrina concluded, "I know you are all somewhat familiar with your job descriptions from the hiring process. Of course it is your responsibility to perform all tasks as you will be trained over the next week. It is equally important, though, that as you perform those tasks you are aware of what is going on around you. It is also your job to greet every guest within 10 feet of you, and yield to them if what you are doing might interfere with their enjoyment of this beautiful facility."

Mr. Safrina's sincere encouragement had inspired the young man. He felt special and welcomed. More importantly, he felt valued.

Mr. Safrina thanked the class and departed. Chai was pleased to see that the next person to speak with them would be Ms. Anati. She handed out a small notebook to each new employee and shared the schedule for their first week at the resort. Chai listened attentively to his new employee orientation plan.

On the first afternoon, he would simply observe experienced landscaping crew members as they worked. This would give him a sense of all of the grounds keeping jobs, not just his role as window washer.

On the second day, Chai would receive training in how to wash windows properly and would practice as his supervisor, Ms. Li, observed and provided feedback. This day was important, she told him, because keeping the windows clean was one of the core tasks he was hired to perform and upon which he would be measured.

On the third day, he would return to the classroom to learn the history of the resort and take a complete tour of the facility. He also would learn more about all of the key performance measurements that Mr. Safrina had mentioned, as well as how each employee makes their unique contribution.

Chai was told that he should take notes in the pocket-sized notebook he was given to carry on him. He would discuss his experiences with Ms. Li at the end of each day. He was asked to specifically note the importance of each job at the resort in maintaining the high standards required to be the finest resort in Brunei.

On the fourth day, he would assume the window washing job, with Ms. Li observing his work. She would score his performance using a checklist in his notebook, with criteria such as cleanliness of the window, time spent, attention to the surrounding area and service to guests.

On the fifth day, all new hires would meet as a group to ask questions and share their experiences. They also would be asked to describe, in their own words, what the resort's mission, to create a great experience for every guest of the Premier Resort, meant to them personally.

The final activity of the week would entail working with Ms. Anati and Ms. Li to create a learning and performance plan for Chai's first year at the resort. "While this week is important," Ms. Anati said, "your ongoing performance and continuing education will be the keys to your success at the Premier Resort."

Amazingly, Chai was told that he would be asked his opinion of the training along the way in order to ensure that he had learned all he needed to learn to be successful and to improve the program for future employees. He couldn't believe that they would want his opinion!

The whole experience was more than Chai had anticipated. Later, he would often point to his first week as one of the reasons for his success and commitment to his job and to the Premier Resort.

Chapter 3
A Dazzled Guest

April 2010
The Premier Resort, Brunei

JIM'S FLIGHT LANDED at the Brunei airport in the middle of the afternoon. Like many other passengers, he was tired from the long flight from the United States. Jim Kirkpatrick, a consultant and author, was accustomed to international travel. Nevertheless, he always found it a bit exhausting.

After passing through customs and reclaiming his bag, he spotted his name spelled out in neat block letters on a sign held by a uniformed town car driver that contained the logo of the Premier Resort. Their eyes met just as Jim broke free from the densest part of the crowd.

"You must be Dr. Kirkpatrick," the resort driver offered in a friendly voice. "How was your flight?"

"Long, but not too bad," Jim returned. "Thanks for asking."

"My pleasure, sir," the driver replied. "My name is Raja. May I help you with your luggage?"

Jim accepted and settled into the meticulously maintained car, soon turning his attention to Raja. A seasoned business traveler, Jim found that professional drivers were sometimes the best source of local information.

He and Raja chatted about the weather forecast for the coming week (beautiful and warm, followed by beautiful and warm) and the amenities and activities offered at the Premier Resort. They briefly discussed the difficulties of travel and Jim's reasons for visiting Brunei.

When they arrived at the resort, Raja offered Jim a business card. "Call if you need a ride anywhere in the city, Dr. Kirkpatrick," he said. Raja unloaded Jim's bags and introduced a uniformed bellman who was waiting nearby. "Dr. Kirkpatrick, this is Leon," Raja said. "He'll take care of you now. I hope you enjoy your stay with us. It was a pleasure to serve you."

Leon continued the fine service by offering up friendly conversation as they made their way through the richly decorated lobby. Beautiful orchids in tall glass vases adorned nearly every available table.

After an efficient check-in experience, Jim learned more about the Premier Resort during his golf cart ride from the lobby to his room. In fact, his driver, Juliana, was so well informed and enthusiastic that Jim would have believed she owned the place. When they discussed the dining options and other amenities offered by the resort, Jim got the impression that the recommendations were based on her actual experiences. Juliana described her favorite menu items and offered to make dinner reservations for Jim or to have a menu sent to his room. By the end of the ride, he was already beginning to feel right at home.

That evening, Jim did indeed follow Juliana's dining recommendation and had a casual dinner at the restaurant overlooking the golf course. It was just what Jim had in mind, and the service was a continuation of the friendly reception he had experienced from all of the resort employees since being picked up at the airport by Raja.

In Jim's consulting and training work, he had stayed in some of the world's most exclusive hotels with the finest service. His international hosts all wanted to show him the very best their countries had to offer. Jim had to admit that the Premier Resort was already on par with the best.

Jim awoke the next morning surprisingly rested and alert, which he attributed to the helpful staff members who got him to his room and then to dinner so efficiently. Looking forward to the class he would be teaching that morning, he made one final review of the course content and then walked across a beautifully landscaped courtyard to the grand lobby in search of breakfast.

As he walked through the lobby, he encountered Juliana, the friendly golf cart driver from the night before. "Good morning, Juliana!" Jim replied. "Say, I wanted to thank you for the restaurant recommendation. It was just perfect."

"I'm glad you enjoyed it," Juliana replied. "Maybe you can help me again," Jim continued, smiling. "Where can I get a glass of juice?"

"Just beyond the main fountain you'll find a beverage station; if you'd like some breakfast, I'd recommend the little bistro café just beyond. You should find it a pleasant place to start your day, as it overlooks a lovely garden," Juliana suggested.

Jim thanked Juliana once again for her advice and headed to the juice bar. He quenched his thirst before heading into the bistro.

Four hours later, after a morning of teaching area trainers how to align their programs with their organizational missions, it was time for lunch. Jim ate another satisfying meal in the company of his course participants and had a bit of time before the afternoon session. He decided to take a walk outside and enjoy the beautiful day. As he made his way down the stairs and outside, he noticed a young man on a step ladder washing windows with a long-handled squeegee. Jim, the friendly sort, made his way over to the young man and greeted him, "Hey, how's it going?"

The young man seemed a bit startled but quickly hopped off his step ladder, stood tall and responded, "Just fine, sir. And how are you?"

"I'm fine. Nice job on your windows."

"Thank you. They do look pretty clean, don't they? Hey, didn't I notice you earlier in that room up there?" He pointed to a bank of windows on the second floor. "It looked like you were speaking to a group of people. Though I was supposed to clean the windows of that room this morning, I decided to wait until after your meeting so I wouldn't disturb you. By the way, my name is Chai."

"Nice to meet you, Chai; I am Dr. Kirkpatrick," said Jim. "It was very thoughtful of you to skip those windows until later."

"My pleasure, Dr. Kirkpatrick. It's part of my responsibility to look out for our guests," Chai responded, and he went on to ask, "When did you arrive?"

"Just yesterday afternoon," Jim said.

"Oh, it got a little cool last night. Did you have enough

blankets and pillows?"

"Yes," Jim responded, thinking to himself, *yes, it must have gotten down to 70 degrees!*

"And did you have a good dinner?"

"Yes, excellent. Thanks for asking." Jim then asked, "What exactly is your job here at the resort, Chai?"

Chai answered, "I am part of a team that creates great experiences for our guests."

Jim was incredulous. How had this young window washer come to respond with such a profound answer? Out of curiosity, Jim asked Chai to tell him more.

For the next few minutes, Chai told Jim how Ms. Anati, Mr. Safrina, Ms. Li and others had helped to orient, train, encourage and coach him. He emphasized the fact that at every step, and with every individual, the ultimate purpose of Chai's role was showcased.

Anyone overhearing this conversation might mistake this young man for one of the resort managers, if not for the 10-foot squeegee pole and resort service staff uniform, Jim thought. *There is something different and special about Chai.* While everyone at the resort treated Jim with kindness, he sensed that Chai really cared that his stay was a pleasant one. Jim soon discovered that his hunch was correct.

Fig. 2 - Chai, the Brunei Window Washer

"Well, Dr. Kirkpatrick," Chai remarked, ending the conversation, "I just wanted to make sure you have everything you need. I won't take any more of your time. I do hope you continue to enjoy your stay with us."

"Thus far, everything has been just fine," Jim replied. "I certainly enjoyed meeting and talking with you. I suppose we should both get back to work."

Chai responded, "Oh, I have been working!"

Chai smiled and turned to walk back to the bank of windows he had been washing. He stopped in his tracks, then quickly turned back to Jim and reengaged him.

"Oh, by the way, Dr. Kirkpatrick," he said. "When you get back to America, will you please tell your friends about the Premier Resort?"

"Sure, Chai," Jim said. "I will be glad to."

Jim started walking through the courtyard, and when he was several steps away, he heard Chai speak again, "And would you please tell them about Brunei?"

My gosh, Jim thought. *This guy not only thinks he is an ambassador for his company, but for his country!*

Chapter 4
A Less Dazzling Experience

April 2010
Four Palms Hotel, Brunei

A DAY LATER, Jim was back at the resort entrance with his luggage, ready to depart for his next destination. It had been a pleasant stay, and he would absolutely follow up on Chai's request to tell people about the Premier Resort and the beautiful country of Brunei.

Jim wished that he could stay longer, but he was on his way to the next business engagement. He was glad that Raja, the friendly driver who had brought him to the resort, would be driving him to the hotel where he would be staying that evening.

When he arrived at the new hotel, Jim thought through his evening agenda. He would check in, shower, grab some dinner and then spend the rest of the evening planning for the next day. By 6:00 pm, he had accomplished the first two items on his list, and he was standing outside the fashionable hotel eager to move on to the next task, finding some dinner.

After his experience at the Premier Resort, Jim unconsciously expected a friendly hotel employee to appear and provide a list of dining recommendations. That hope was quickly dashed when he left the front desk holding a slip of paper noting the name and address of the closest restaurant.

He stepped outside the front entrance to find a taxi to take him to the unfamiliar destination. Unfortunately, he discovered that a taxi was a scarce commodity. After standing alone in front of the hotel for five minutes watching occupied taxis whiz by, Jim realized he needed some assistance.

Surprised by the absence of even a bellman, Jim was glad to see a hotel employee who happened to be cleaning a window in front of the hotel. *Great*, he thought. *Maybe this is someone friendly and knowledgeable, like Chai.* Hopeful, he walked over to the worker, calling to him from a short distance away.

"Hi, I was wondering if you know how to get a taxi," Jim said. "Am I in the right place?"

"I don't know," the tired-eyed young man replied.

Jim decided to take another approach. "Is someone responsible for getting taxis for hotel guests?"

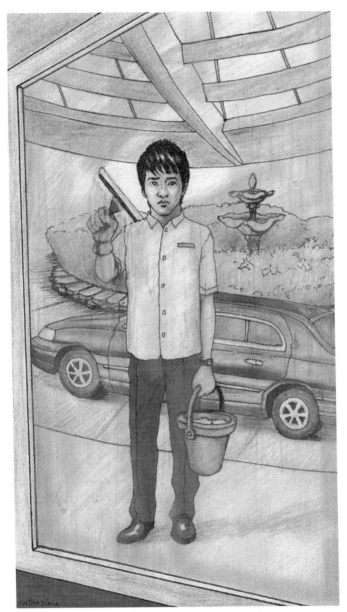

Fig. 3 - The Unhappy Window Washer

The young man continued to look at his window and said, "I don't know."

"Do you suppose someone inside might know?" Jim replied, now with a bit of frustration.

"Perhaps," the window washer replied.

Jim turned to walk back inside. *Surely,* he thought, *some other employee will be more helpful than this window washer.* He took a few steps away from the scene but turned back to ask one last question, trying not to sound sarcastic.

"Excuse me, but what is your job here at the hotel?"

The young man dunked his squeegee into a bucket of soapy water, and without even looking up, he replied, "I am a window washer."

Later that evening, with both dinner and workshop preparation checked off his list, Jim reflected on his day. He was struck by the contrast between the Four Palms Hotel and the Premier Resort, particularly the vast difference between the two window washers. *It is so interesting how two similarly aged men performing the same task in the same country could answer the same question so differently.*

Chai was an extraordinary employee, but the window washer at this hotel was unremarkable, Jim thought. *When I get back to my office next week,* he mused, *I will write to the general manager of the Premier Resort and let him know how impressed I was with the resort and all the employees, in particular the young window washer named Chai.*

Jim did not see the unhappy window washer again during his visit at the Four Palms. The window washer, in fact, was not employed at the hotel much longer. He saw an ad for a window washer position at the Grand Palace and thought he might get paid a little more. He applied and was immediately hired based on his past experience.

Chapter 5
An Extraordinary
Employee Gets Even Better

June 2010
Premier Resort

TWO MONTHS HAD passed since Chai's conversation
with Jim. His confidence continued to grow with each
guest interaction. Both Ms. Anati and Ms. Li checked
in with him on a regular basis to make sure he had
everything he needed to perform successfully and
maintain his commitment to a great guest experience.
They tracked his performance by auditing his cleaned
windows and observing his guest interactions.

Chai made a point of knowing as much as he could
about the resort and grounds. He kept track of special
groups and conventions. Guests seemed to appreciate
his knowledge and friendly attitude; for Chai, an
enthusiastic 'thank you' was reward enough for his
efforts. However, his spirit did not go unnoticed by his
team members at the resort.

Due to his performance, Chai had received a raise and additional responsibilities on the landscaping team, so he now had many jobs in addition to washing windows. Some days he spent mowing the lawn, others working with landscapers to plant new beds of flowers. Chai took every job seriously. He never lost sight of the fact that making every guest experience positive was his biggest job at the resort.

Ms. Li often observed Chai as he worked and commented on the quality of his work and his dedication. She took an active part in developing Chai for increasing levels of responsibility. She also cared about him as a person, often asking about his well-being and that of his family.

Sometimes Ms. Li suggested a better way for Chai to perform a certain task or corrected him if he made a mistake. Chai never took the suggestions as criticism. *After all*, he thought, *we're on the same team and she tells me how to improve because she wants me to be successful.*

Chai was happy to be part of the landscaping team. He willingly switched shifts when his co-workers needed a day off, and volunteered to mentor new team members. His reputation as one of the most cooperative team members was not lost on Ms. Li.

Chapter 6
An Unexpected Phone
Call

April 2011
Jim's office

IT HAD BEEN nearly a year since Jim had written
to the general manager of the Premier Resort. While
sending an e-mail would have been more efficient, he
had decided that a posted letter showed just how much
he valued his time at the resort.

In the note, Jim had described his interactions with the
resort employees he had come to know. He mentioned
Raja, who picked him up at the airport, described the
helpful dining suggestions from Juliana, and praised
the food and service at the restaurants. But Jim saved
his highest praise to describe the most impressive resort
employee of all, Chai the window washer.

He ended the letter, "I know that the one of your core
values is to exceed customer expectations. Chai's actions
raised the Premier Resort to that level and beyond for

me. When I come back to Brunei, I will be staying with you. So will my friends and colleagues. Please share this note with Chai and thank him again for me. Your resort is fortunate to have him as an employee."

A few weeks after sending the letter, Jim received a nice response from Mr. Safrina. The manager had used an old style fountain pen to compose the note. *An elegant touch*, Jim thought. In the letter, Mr. Safrina thanked Jim, noting that he was glad the Premier Resort guest service values had been so well represented by the staff. Mr. Safrina assured Jim that he would share the letter with Chai. He also agreed that Chai was a remarkable and valued employee whose customer service was well known by both the resort's management and staff.

When Jim received a phone call from Brunei nearly a year later, he was surprised to find that it was the manager of the Premier Resort.

"Nice to hear from you, Mr. Safrina," Jim replied.

Mr. Safrina thanked Jim again for his letter and told him about an upcoming employee recognition and promotion ceremony. He said that Chai was to be promoted to supervisor and that he would be receiving additional recognition as part of the event. He noted that Jim's letter had played a part in those decisions.

"Is there any chance that you could write up a brief note that I could read to Chai when he is presented his award?" Mr. Safrina asked Jim.

"Actually," Jim responded, "I can do better than that. I am going to be in Southeast Asia the day of your event, and I would be honored to say a few words at the ceremony. That is, if you would like that."

"Like it?" Mr. Safrina exclaimed. "That would be stupendous. I couldn't even have asked for that, and I know it will make the evening so special for Chai."

About a month before Mr. Safrina had called Jim, Ms. Li had spotted Chai policing the resort's entrance gardens.

"Hi Chai," she had said. "I didn't expect to see you working so late today."

"Yes, Ms. Li," Chai replied. "I was just on my way home, and I noticed some yard waste in this garden. I just stopped to pick it up."

This wasn't the first time Ms. Li had observed Chai going the extra mile for his job. She saw him speaking to guests regularly and knew that he encouraged and coached other team members to do the same.

Ms. Li had been delighted when Mr. Safrina shared the letter he received from Jim at their weekly manager meeting. Her face particularly brightened when he read the part about Chai. After the meeting, Mr. Safrina talked privately with Ms. Li and Ms. Anati and asked if either had given thought to supervisory training for Chai.

"Yes," Ms. Li told him. "I was planning to ask Ms. Anati to enroll him in the next round. I'm so pleased you agree that this is the right move."

The next day, Ms. Li had interrupted Chai as he carefully cleaned a set of windows. She thanked Chai again for his extra efforts at the resort gate. As she did so, she handed him a copy of the letter from Dr. Kirkpatrick. As Chai read it, his smile grew broader with each sentence.

"I do remember Dr. Kirkpatrick," Chai said. "It was very nice of him to write, and I am glad to know his name once again. But you know it's the same way I treat all of our guests. Making customers happy is just part of my job."

"I know," Ms. Li said, "and that's what makes you so special. That's why I'm pleased to tell you that you will be attending supervisor training starting next month. That is, if you are interested."

"Yes!" Chai answered excitedly.

Ms. Li returned to her office and began completing the paperwork.

Chapter 7
A Day of Celebration

May 2011
The Grand Palace

CHAI PACED IN the foyer outside the ballroom where the awards ceremony would begin in just a few minutes. He thought walking would relax him, so he had left the table where he had been seated with his co-workers. Chai saw Mr. Safrina enter the ballroom talking with a foreign-looking man who Chai thought he recognized but couldn't place. He didn't have long to ponder; the sound of the ballroom doors closing summoned him back to his seat.

Chai slipped into the ballroom just moments before the festivities began. First, a traditional dance and music troupe performed on a large stage set up for the event. Then, after a fine meal, the general manager took the stage to welcome everyone. He made a few opening remarks about the importance of guest service and reminded the audience again of the benefits it brings to the resort. It was a message that Chai had always taken to heart.

Mr. Safrina then called Chai and a number of other resort employees onto the stage. Each was honored with a framed certificate and thunderous applause for being promoted within the last year. Chai was so proud of his certificate. *I will show this to my parents and then hang it on my wall,* he thought.

The ceremony then continued with various service awards. Chai was curious to see if any of his friends would receive one of them. He thought Ms. Li deserved an award, and Ms. Anati as well. Chai clapped enthusiastically as each recipient approached the stage. He was genuinely happy to see his co-workers receive recognition.

As Chai watched the awards on the skirted table dwindle, he began to worry that Ms. Li would not be recognized. He had watched the award presentations for outstanding guest service, sales and best manager leave Ms. Li sitting at her table. Finally, a single glass statue remained. Chai crossed his fingers that the final award was for Ms. Li.

"I know we have given many awards tonight," Mr. Safrina said as picked up the lone glass statue, "but this final award is very special because it's for the Employee of the Year." Chai sat up, hopeful for Ms. Li once again.

He sat on the edge of his seat in anticipation of the big

announcement. At the same time, Jim was preparing himself to address the group about the importance of exceptional customer service, ultimately presenting Chai as his star example. Jim had noticed Chai's puzzled expression when he glanced in his direction before the ceremony. It made him worry that Chai had figured out the big surprise. *No matter,* he thought. *Chai will have his moment soon enough.*

When Jim heard the key phrase that he and Mr. Safrina had agreed would serve as his cue, "but we have one more award to give," he slid his chair back, gathered his notes, stood up and walked to the podium.

Mr. Safrina introduced the man, whose face Chai had tried to place all evening. He told the audience that the speaker, Dr. Jim Kirkpatrick, had come all the way from America to be part of the awards ceremony. He said Dr. Kirkpatrick was directly connected to the final award. That's when it hit Chai; the face belonged to the man he had met while washing windows who had written the nice letter to Mr. Safrina.

Chai paid close attention to what Dr. Kirkpatrick was saying. He especially liked the part about how important it is to have training and how training is connected to great customer service. He also related to Dr. Kirkpatrick's comments about connecting all associates to the true mission of the resort. But mostly, Chai tried to figure out the why this particular guest was invited above all other guests who had visited the resort; then he got the surprising answer.

"Ms. Li," Jim asked, "would you please join us on stage?"

The invitation jarred Chai from his distracted thoughts. He was sure he had the answer. *The American guest has come to give Ms. Li the Employee of the Year award*, he concluded, accenting the conclusion with a burst of clapping that was echoed by the other ballroom guests.

Ms. Li mounted the stage and stood next to Mr. Safrina; Jim approached the podium to speak again. Chai expected him to begin telling the audience why Ms. Li had been chosen as employee of the year; but instead, Jim recounted the day he had met an extraordinary resort employee washing windows.

Chai couldn't believe it. He realized the American guest was talking about him! The next few minutes passed in a blur.

"I am most pleased to present this final and most prestigious award of the evening," Mr. Safrina said. "Our employee of the year for 2010 is Chai! Chai, please join us on the stage."

Chai momentarily froze but managed to stand up. As he walked to the stage amidst a standing ovation from his co-workers, he felt like he was floating. It was a feeling he had never before experienced.

Mr. Safrina approached Chai to hand him the beautiful glass statue and offer a hearty handshake and

congratulations. Chai and Ms. Li wiped tears away
with the backs of their hands.

Mr. Safrina asked if Chai had anything he would like
to say to his co-workers. After all, they had been part of
the selection process as well. Although he was nervous
and choked with emotion, Chai found the strength to
share what was in his heart:

"Thank you all so much for this honor. I am so happy.
Thank you for the faith you have all shown in me. But
I have to say, this resort makes it easy for anyone who
wants to succeed. From the first day I met Ms. Li and
Mr. Safrina, I felt respected and valued. My job was
recognized as being important to the success of the
resort. I never thought of my job in any other way."

"When I was hired as a window washer here," Chai
continued, "it was a great day. I came to the job thinking
that I would be the best window washer the Premier
Resort had ever seen, and I worked toward that goal.
But more than my work, my managers and co-workers
made my success possible," Chai said.

"Ms. Li worked with me to set goals, and I always knew
what it would take to accomplish them. She taught me,
and some days challenged me and corrected me. And I
can't forget the other people on the maintenance team.
We are always there for each other, double checking
each other's work and making sure that everything is
up to standard for our guests. It's easy to see why we
all succeed."

Fig. 4 - Jim Kirkpatrick and Chai

Chai finished his heartfelt speech to more applause from his co-workers. Jim approached him by crossing the stage with one final surprise.

"Chai," Jim said, "I was so impressed with you, your resort and your country that I wrote a book about it, and here it is." Jim handed Chai a copy of the book, then smiled. "I'll be glad to sign it for you if you wish." The crowd laughed appreciatively.

Chai was truly speechless as he cradled the small book in his arms. There was a caricature that strongly resembled him featured on the cover.

"A book about me," he marveled out loud. "I really don't know what to say. Thank you!"

"No, thank *you*," Jim countered. "You have no idea how many people your story will help to achieve the same success you are enjoying this evening."

With that, Chai wiped away another tear. He and Jim left the stage to a final standing ovation in honor of Chai.

Chapter 8
A New General
Manager's Challenge

February 2008
The Premier Resort

MR. SAFRINA WALKED slowly, surveying the grounds of his newest and greatest challenge – the Premier Resort and Hotel in his beloved country of Brunei. Being chosen to serve as the General Manager filled him with pride, and he couldn't wait to help make this the best resort in all of Asia.

Mr. Safrina was tempted to immediately implement numerous ideas he had crafted and fine-tuned over the past several years in other positions throughout Southeast Asia. After all, he was no longer the manager of a small property or a single department; he was now manager of an entire resort. He caught himself, however, and decided that he would curtail his enthusiasm long enough to get the lay of the land. He knew he would supply the spark and direction for positive change, but it would ultimately be his leaders and employees who would breathe life into the new culture.

As Mr. Safrina made his way around the property, he did a lot of watching and listening. He noticed the cut of the fairway grass on the championship golf course, the way the tables were set in the dining room and the cleanliness of the grounds and buildings.

He was most keenly focused, however, on the behaviors of his new staff. While he saw and heard politeness and professionalism from most team members, there was something missing. Mr. Safrina thought for a moment, and then he deduced that there was a lack of passion in their voices and actions. While this was somewhat discouraging, he did notice pockets of excellence, like openings in the clouds during a brilliant sunset. *Soon enough*, he thought, *every member of this resort staff will be like those bright spots in the sky to our guests.*

Mr. Safrina began asking many questions of staff members in all areas of the resort. He asked about their experiences and, perhaps more importantly, their outlook. He observed employee behavior in the mailroom, throughout the lobby, and on all areas of the grounds. He even studied the window washers, recalling his own first job at the age of 16.

Mr. Safrina observed the guests just as keenly. *What are they doing? What are they thinking? How are they feeling about being here?* he thought. He also spoke with a number of guests about their experiences at the resort. Mr. Safrina concluded that overall the guests were somewhat underwhelmed with the resort, though they had few specific complaints. Again, he thought, *Soon enough they will see what real guest service looks and feels like!*

Mr. Safrina had gathered enough information to be able to take action intelligently. While it was tempting to simply offer training and implement a leadership model designed to correct the shortcomings he observed, he wanted to try something different. It would be the responsibility of every employee to create and nurture a new, customer-focused culture, so he would involve individuals from every department and level to design and execute the new vision.

The culture change began with Mr. Safrina inviting top performers he identified during his observations to participate in round table discussions. During these meetings, Mr. Safrina shared his vision, results from recent guest surveys and employee exit interviews, and he solicited ideas for improvement.

A new guest service plan was developed based on the round table discussions and resort data. The formula for success included targets for guest satisfaction, employee retention, guest referrals and overall revenue. This plan provided for training, on-the-job learning, supervisory reinforcement, peer-to-peer coaching, mentoring, recognition, executive modeling, evaluation, systems of accountability and personal responsibility.

The plan was implemented and began taking effect at

the Premier Resort over the new few months. It was not without a few bumps in the road, so to speak. Some employees, happy to be complacent, did not enjoy the added time in training and observation from their manager and peers. They quickly departed, in favor of employment at less challenging organizations. Mr. Safrina coached his management team to understand that sometimes a bit of turnover is good and necessary to change a culture. Overall, the plan was going quite smoothly, and everyone came to look at the gains on all metrics posted weekly on the dashboard as a compass for continual improvement.

A special recognition event was held six months after implementation of the guest service plan to recognize managers and employees who best exemplified the true spirit of the new culture and exhibited high guest service and revenue ratings to match. As Mr. Safrina watched the smiles of satisfaction and pride from longtime managers, including Ms. Li and Ms. Anati, he knew they were well-equipped for a long and successful ride together.

While Mr. Safrina planned no closing speech for the first recognition event, he couldn't contain himself from proclaiming, "It is indeed an honor and pleasure to work with people such as all of you. I entrust you to help bring the rest of our employees along this journey with us. We are all part of the team that creates great experiences for our guests!"

**Chapter 9
The Next Brunei
Window Washer?**

June 2011
The Premier Resort

THE UNHAPPY WINDOW washer who Jim had
encountered at The Four Palms Resort would never
know the inadvertent positive impact of his poor
customer service habits. Unbeknownst to him, it was
his dismissive attitude that gave Jim the idea to write to
the Premier Resort to commend Chai on his exemplary
performance.

Since meeting Jim, the unhappy window washer had
been traveling 45 minutes per day to his job, now at
the Grand Palace hotel. Even though the wages were
better than at the Four Palms, he was tired of the long,
hot bus ride to work each day. He started looking for a
new position closer to home.

He heard there may be a window washer opening at the
best resort in Brunei. Better yet, it was only a short bike

ride from his home.

The next day, the unhappy window washer called in sick to his job and rode his bike to the Premier Resort. He filled out an application that seemed longer than required for a service job. He checked boxes and circled numbers next to many questions and statements about his career goals, likes and dislikes, and what kinds of people he worked with best.

The simplest question on the form asked why he was applying for work at the resort. The correct answer was one of the choices provided. He placed a deliberate check mark in the box next to the statement, "I need a job." He handed the completed forms to the hiring manager with somewhat of a sigh, feeling a bit put out by the effort.

The hiring manager, Ms. Anati, quickly looked over the forms and opened the conversation with, "So Benji, I see that you like washing windows."

The young man did not recall checking any boxes indicating that he liked washing windows. *Still*, Benji thought, *I could really use this job. I'll answer positively and maybe she'll hire me.* He sat up slightly from his slouched position and tried to look interested.

"Yes," he replied to Ms. Anati. "That's what I do. I am a window washer."

"Very well," Ms. Anati said, sensing some indifference

from her interviewee. "What is your favorite thing about the job?"

"Um, I guess I would say if I got this job, that my ride to work would be a lot shorter, so work wouldn't take up all of my time," said Benji.

That's the most enthusiasm I've seen out of this candidate, Ms. Anati thought with dismay. She decided to take a different approach.

"What questions do you have for me, Benji?" Ms. Anati asked warmly.

Benji, taken aback that a manager would want to hear his thoughts, stammered for a moment, then asked, "What's it like to work here?"

"Well, Benji, it's different than some other resorts. We believe that each and every employee is part of a team that helps to create great experiences for our guests. This means that each person is equally important."

Benji couldn't believe what he was hearing. "Really?" he asked.

"Yes," said Ms. Anati.

"That must be really great. I mean, you are asking me questions and really taking the time to listen to me. I don't really remember that happening in jobs I have had. Even the one I have now," Benji said.

"That's too bad," said Ms. Anati. "I bet they could have learned a lot from you based on your close interactions with guests on a daily basis."

"Oh, we weren't really supposed to speak with the customers," Benji said. "If someone asked us a question, we were supposed to send them to the front desk or tell them where to find a courtesy telephone," he said. "It sounds like you do things differently here."

"Yes, we do," Ms. Anati said with a laugh. "That's why we consistently win customer service awards and have a high rate of return visitors. Many of our guests even remember their favorite employees by name."

"Wow, that would be really great," said Benji. "How do your employees learn how to give the customers the right answers about things?" he asked with honesty.

"We have a full week of orientation for every associate, and on-the-job training that continues for an employee's entire career. We believe that learning is part of the job because we can see how it enhances performance. That performance is what makes our guests so happy here, and that's what keeps us in business. It's a great system."

"Ms. Anati, this really sounds like a special place. If you were to give me a chance, I know I'm an excellent window washer, and I would really like to give being a Premier Resort team member a try. I can learn new things," Benji said.

"I'm pleased to hear that you are still interested in the position after hearing more about it," Ms. Anati said with a smile. "I have a few other people to interview, but I will get back to you personally by the end of the week to let you know how we will move forward," she said.

"Thank you for considering me, Ms. Anati. I would work very hard for you, and for the guests here at the resort. I am ready for a new challenge," Benji said.

Ms. Anati and Benji shook hands, and Benji departed. Ms. Anati completed her interview notes with the comment. "We may have found our next Chai."

Part II: The
Kirkpatrick
Methodology

"Try not to become a man of
success, but rather try to become
a man of value."

Albert Einstein

The story in Part I was written to stir your heart and stimulate your mind. Indeed, there are many other employees like Chai; you may know (or be) one of them. Each has found the path to live beyond his or her own needs and impact the lives of those around them. They contribute to the greater good.

You have undoubtedly encountered one or more employees like Chai, often when you least expect it. Take a moment to remember what it was like and the impact it had on your day, and possibly your life.

In this section, the methodology that underpins the story is explained to better illustrate how the Premier Resort accomplished success through business partnership. Examples from the story are correlated to the principles.

Any organization can enjoy the same level of accomplishment explained in this book by systematically applying the principles in this section. Recommendations for implementation are included in Part III – Getting Started.

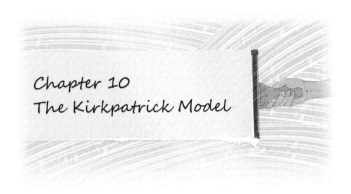

Chapter 10
The Kirkpatrick Model

THE KIRKPATRICK MODEL was developed by Dr. Donald Kirkpatrick in the mid-1950s as he wrote his Ph.D. dissertation. His goal was to effectively measure the impact of the management development programs he taught at the University of Wisconsin Management Institute.

Dr. Kirkpatrick, Sr.'s, work became known and later published by a trade journal in the late 1950s. Over the following 50 years, worldwide use grew organically.

Today, the Kirkpatrick Model is the most highly recognized, utilized and regarded method of evaluating the effectiveness of training programs.

In 2010, Dr. Kirkpatrick, Sr.'s, son, Jim, and daughter-in-law, Wendy, enhanced the Kirkpatrick Model to accomplish the following goals:

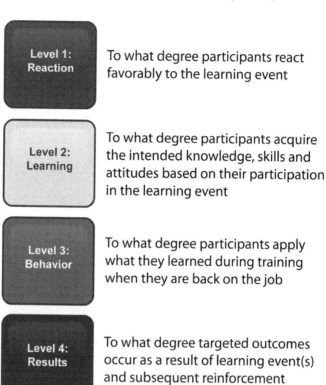

Fig. 5 - The Kirkpatrick Model

- Incorporate the forgotten or overlooked teachings of Dr. Kirkpatrick, Sr.
- Correct common misinterpretations and misuse of the model
- Illustrate how the model applies to modern workplace learning and performance

The New World Kirkpatrick Model honors and maintains the time-tested four levels and adds new elements to help people to operationalize it effectively.

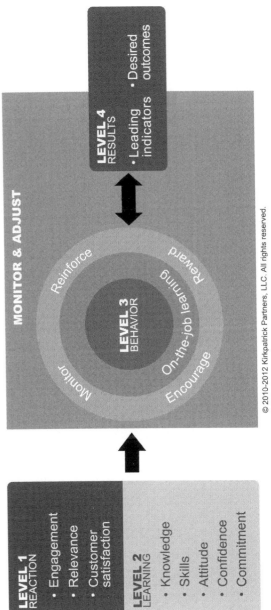

Fig. 6 - The New World Kirkpatrick Model

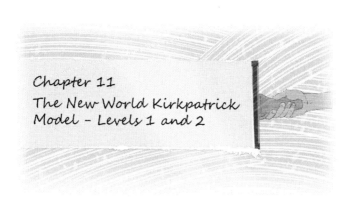

Chapter 11
The New World Kirkpatrick
Model – Levels 1 and 2

THIS CHAPTER OUTLINES Levels 1 and 2 of the New World Kirkpatrick Model, referred to as "effective training." These levels measure the quality of the training and the degree to which it resulted in knowledge and skills that can be applied on the job.

These measurements are useful primarily to the training function to internally measure the quality of the programs they design and deliver.

Level 1: Reaction

Level 1 Reaction is the degree to which participants react favorably to the learning event.

Level 1	Level 2	Level 3	Level 4
Reaction	Learning	Behavior	Results

> ## Level 1: Reaction
> The degree to which participants react favorably to the learning event

Approximately 78% of training events measure Level 1 Reaction in some fashion. The current investment in gathering this type of data is far greater than the importance this level dictates. This investment occurs at the cost of measuring Levels 3 and 4, which would yield data more meaningful to the business; these levels are only measured 25% and 15% of the time, respectively (American Society of Training and Development (ASTD) "Value of Evaluation," 2009).

The New World Kirkpatrick Level 1 Reaction has three dimensions: customer satisfaction, relevance and engagement.

Customer Satisfaction

The original definition of Level 1 measured only participant satisfaction with the training. Dr. Kirkpatrick, Sr., referred to this as the customer satisfaction measurement of training.

Examples from the Story

Chapter 2 describes Chai's new employee orientation and training. He is asked throughout the process for his feedback on the experience:

Chai was told that he should take notes in the pocket-sized notebook he was given to carry on him. He would discuss his experiences with Ms. Li at the end of each day.

On the fifth day (of orientation) all new hires would meet as a group to ask questions and share their experiences.

Amazingly, Chai was told that he would be asked his opinion of the training along the way in order to ensure that he had learned all he needed to learn to be successful and to improve the program for future employees.

Engagement

Engagement refers to the degree to which participants are actively involved in and contributing to the learning experience. Engagement levels directly relate to the level of learning that is attained.

Personal responsibility and program interest are both factors in the measurement of engagement. Personal responsibility relates to how "present" and attentive participants are during the training. Program interest is more commonly the focus, including how the facilitator involved and captivated the audience.

Examples from the Story

When using the four levels to monitor and measure training, the same tool or exercise often can measure multiple levels and dimensions simultaneously.

The small notebook given to Chai and the discussion with Ms. Li about his notes and experiences at the end of each day also serve to measure his level of engagement throughout the process.

Relevance

Relevance is the degree to which training participants will have the opportunity to use or apply what they learned in training on the job.

Relevance is important to ultimate training value because even the best training is a waste of resources if the participants have no application for the content in their everyday work.

Examples from the Story

The Premier Resort explained the relevance of the training program and Chai's future role in the overall success of the resort throughout the hiring and training process.

Ms. Anati told Chai during his interview:

*"Whether you cook, clean or wash the windows, yo[u]
part of a larger team that is responsible for creating great
experiences for our guests," she had told Chai. "Your face-to-
face interaction is what really brings the spirit of the resort,
and Brunei, to life for them."*

*Mr. Safrina opened the new employee orientation by saying,
"I am here this morning to personally welcome you to our
team and to tell you just how important your jobs are to me,
the other employees of this resort, and especially our guests."*

*Ms. Li continued to check that Chai understood the relevance
of what he was learning to his new role at the resort.*

Level 1 Summary

Level 1 is the most often measured level, yet the least
important in terms of obtaining data that are relevant
to the value of training to the organization.

Level 1 measurements include the relevance of the
material to the learner's job function, the learner's
engagement in the training, and customer satisfaction,
or the learner's overall reaction to the program.

Level 1 data is useful primarily to the training function
as internal quality control measurements.

Level 2: Learning

The original definition of Level 2 Learning is the degree to which participants acquire the intended knowledge, skills and attitudes based on their participation in the learning event.

Level 1   **Level 2**   Level 3   Level 4
Reaction   **Learning**   Behavior   Results

Level 2: Learning

To what degree participants acquire the intended knowledge, skills and attitudes based on their participation in the learning event

Two new dimensions, confidence and commitment, have been added to Level 2 in the New World Model. These dimensions help to close the gap between learning and behavior and to prevent the cycle of waste when training is repeated for people who possess the required knowledge and skills but fail to perform appropriately on the job.

Knowledge and Skill

Knowledge is the degree to which participants know certain information, as characterized by the phrase, "I know it." Skill is the degree to which they know how to do something or perform a certain task, as illustrated by the phrase, "I can do it right now."

A common and costly mistake many organizations make is inaccurately diagnosing poor performance as a lack of knowledge or skill. Underachievers are continually returned to training with the belief that they do not know what to do, when in reality the more common cause of substandard performance is a lack of motivation or other environmental factors.

Only about 10% of learning transfer failure (i.e., a training graduate failing to perform new skills on the job) is due to training; 70% or more of such failure is due to something in the application environment (State of the Industry: ASTD's Annual Review of Trends in Workplace Learning and Performance, ASTD, 2006).

Examples from the Story

The Premier Resort had implemented a good plan to ensure that Chai had knowledge of the resort and the skill to wash windows and provide excellent customer service:

On the second day, Chai would receive training in how to wash windows properly and would practice as his supervisor, Ms. Li, observed and provided feedback.

On the third day, he would return to the classroom to learn the history of the resort and take a complete tour of the facility. He also would learn more about all of the key performance measurements that Mr. Safrina had mentioned, as well as how each employee makes their unique contribution.

Attitude

Attitude is defined as the degree to which training participants believe that it will be worthwhile to implement what is learned during training on the job.

Attitude is characterized by the phrase, "I believe it will be worthwhile" (to do this in my work).

Examples from the Story

The Premier Resort incorporated a formal measurement of attitude into their new employee orientation:

On the fifth day, all new hires would meet as a group to ask questions and share their experiences. They also would be asked to describe, in their own words, what the resort's mission, to create a great experience for every guest of the Premier Resort, meant to them personally.

Note once again that multiple dimensions can be measured with the same measurement episode or tool, in this case, customer satisfaction and attitude. Based on trainee comments, levels of knowledge and engagement possibly also could be ascertained.

Confidence

Confidence is defined as the degree to which training participants think they will be able to do what they learned during training on the job. It is characterized by the question, "I think I can do it on the job."

Addressing confidence during training brings learners closer to the desired on-the-job performance. It can proactively surface potential on-the-job application barriers so they can be resolved.

Examples from the Story

Ms. Li informally measured Chai's confidence during his training as part of the conversation that occurred at the end of each day as they reviewed the notes he made in his small notebook.

Chai's confidence was measured more formally at the end of the first week:

Amazingly, Chai was told that he would be asked his opinion of the training along the way in order to ensure that he had learned all he needed to learn to be successful..."

Ms. Li continued to monitor Chai's level of confidence with questions during the work reviews that occurred during his first weeks of employment.

Commitment

Commitment is defined as the degree to which learners intend to apply the knowledge and skills learned during training to their jobs. It is characterized by the phrase, "I intend to do it on the job."

Commitment relates to learner motivation by

acknowledging that even if the knowledge and skills are mastered, effort still must be put forth to use the information or perform the skills on a daily basis.

Examples from the Story

Ms. Li and Ms. Anati measured Chai's commitment with regular conversations on the topic:

Two months had passed since Chai's conversation with Jim. His confidence continued to grow with each guest interaction. Both Ms. Anati and Ms. Li checked in with him on a regular basis to make sure he had everything he needed to perform successfully and maintain his commitment to a great guest experience.

Level 2 Summary

Measuring knowledge, skill, attitude, confidence and commitment during and after training provides the necessary data to show that effective training has occurred. It also focuses interventions on the correct root causes of performance problems so they can be solved efficiently.

Complete Level 2 data can reduce the cycle of waste that occurs when training is repeated over and over again due to the belief that substandard on-the-job performance is caused by a lack of knowledge and skill, when in reality it is a condition in the work environment or a learner motivation issue.

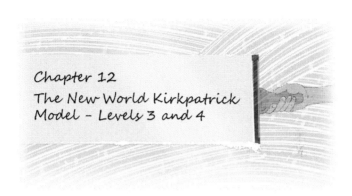

Chapter 12
The New World Kirkpatrick
Model - Levels 3 and 4

THIS CHAPTER OUTLINES Levels 3 and 4, referred to as "training effectiveness." Training effectiveness encompasses:

- On-the-job performance and subsequent business results that occur, in part, due to training and reinforcement
- Demonstration of the value that the training has contributed to the organization

Level 3: Behavior

Level 3 is the degree to which participants apply what they learned during training when they are back on the job.

Level 1	Level 2	Level 3	Level 4
Reaction	Learning	**Behavior**	Results

> **Level 3 Behavior**
>
> The degree to which participants apply what they learned during training when they are back on the job

The New World Level 3 Behavior consists of critical behaviors, required drivers and on-the-job learning.

Critical Behaviors

Critical behaviors are the few, specific actions, which if performed consistently on the job, will have the biggest impact on the desired results.

> **Critical Behaviors**
>
> The few, specific actions, which if performed consistently on the job, will have the biggest impact on the desired results

There are perhaps thousands of behaviors a given employee might perform on the job; critical behaviors are those that have been identified as the most important to achieving organizational success.

Examples from the Story

At the Premier Resort, each employee had one critical behavior in common: to address all guests within 10 feet of them and ask them about their stay. Mr. Safrina explained this on the first day of orientation:

"Of course it is your responsibility to perform all tasks as you will be trained over the next week. It is equally important, though, that as you perform those tasks you are aware of what is going on around you. It is also your job to greet each guest within 10 feet of you, and yield to them if what you are doing might interfere with their enjoyment of this beautiful facility."

Every employee at the resort also had one or two other critical behaviors (referred to as core tasks) specific to their job:

On the second day, Chai would receive training in how to wash windows properly and would practice as his supervisor, Ms. Li, observed and provided feedback. This day was important, she told him, because keeping the windows clean was one of the core tasks he was hired to perform and upon which he would be measured.

Required Drivers

The New World Kirkpatrick Model adds required drivers to Level 3. Required drivers are processes and systems that reinforce, monitor, encourage and reward performance of the critical behaviors on the job.

Required Drivers

Processes and systems that reinforce, monitor, encourage and reward performance of critical behaviors on the job

Organizations that reinforce the knowledge and skills learned during training with accountability and support systems can expect as much as 85% application on the job. Conversely, companies that rely primarily on training events alone to create good job performance achieve around a 15% success rate (R.O. Brinkerhoff, *Telling Training's Story*).

Required drivers are the key to accomplishing the desired on-the-job application of what is learned during training. They decrease the likelihood of people falling through the cracks or deliberately crawling through the cracks if they are not interested in performing the required behaviors.

Active execution and monitoring of required drivers is perhaps the biggest indicator of program success for any initiative.

SUPPORT

Reinforce
- Follow-up modules
- Work review checklist
- On-the-job training (OJT)
- Self-directed learning
- Refreshers
- Job aids
- Reminders
- Executive modeling

Encourage
- Coaching
- Mentoring

Reward
- Recognition
- Bonuses
- Pay for performance

ACCOUNTABILITY

Monitor
- Action learning
- Interviews
- Observation
- Self monitoring
- Key performance indicators (KPIs)

- Action planning
- Dashboard
- Work review
- Survey

Fig. 7 - Required Drivers

Examples from the Story

Chai's first days of work were filled with monitoring:

On the fourth day, he would assume the window washing job, with Ms. Li observing his work. She would score his performance using a checklist in his notebook, with criteria such as cleanliness of the window, time spent, attention to the surrounding area and service to guests.

Intermittent monitoring continued throughout his job, incorporating reinforcement and encouragement:

Ms. Li often observed Chai as he worked and commented on the quality of his work and his dedication. She took an active part in developing Chai for increasing levels of responsibility.

Sometimes Ms. Li suggested a better way for Chai to perform a certain task or corrected him if he made a mistake. Chai never took the suggestions as criticism. After all, he thought, we're on the same team and she tells me how to improve because she wants me to be successful.

The Premier Resort used a dashboard as an efficient way to tie together multiple drivers:

You will see updated statistics each week on a poster like this in the employee break area." Mr. Safrina held up an example (of a dashboard).

Continual monitoring, reinforcement and encouragement provided the basis for Chai to be rightfully rewarded for his good performance:

Due to his performance, Chai had received a raise and additional responsibilities on the landscaping team, so he now had many jobs in addition to washing windows.

Chai was also publicly rewarded for his efforts:

> *"I am most pleased to present this final and most prestigious award of the evening," Mr. Safrina said. "Our employee of the year for 2010 is Chai! Chai, please join us on the stage."*

On-the-Job Learning

On-the-job learning also has been added as a New World dimension of Level 3 in recognition of two facts of the modern workplace:

1. Up to 70% of all learning takes place on the job
2. Personal responsibility and motivation are key partners to external support and reinforcement efforts for optimal performance

Creating a culture and expectation that individuals are responsible for maintaining the knowledge and skills to enhance their own performance will encourage individuals to be accountable and feel empowered.

On-the-job learning provides an opportunity for employees and their employers to share the responsibility for good performance.

Level 3 Summary

Level 3 includes more than measurement and evaluation activities. While these are reflected in the monitoring dimension of required drivers, reinforcing, encouraging and rewarding proper behavior also must occur for maximum organizational results.

Examples from the Story

The Premier Resort set the expectation for ongoing learning during employee orientation:

The final activity of the week would be working with Ms. Anati and Ms. Li to create a learning and performance plan for Chai's first year at the resort.

In Chapter 5, Chai refers to his responsibility for continuing his learning:

He made a point of knowing as much as he could about the resort and grounds. He kept track of special groups and conventions.

The importance of Level 3 is punctuated by its representation as a bulls-eye in the center of the New World Kirkpatrick Model. Despite its importance in accomplishing organizational results, execution tends to be weak overall.

Common excuses for not performing Level 3 activities include:

- It's too difficult
- It's too expensive
- It isn't our job (in the training department)
- Business managers won't support it

Based on the variety of required drivers available, it is neither difficult nor expensive to execute a Level 3 support plan. Training and business professionals together should review the learning transfer statistics and come to an agreement during the planning stage of an initiative to determine who will perform and measure each driver.

Program plans for major initiatives that overlook any of the four dimensions of required drivers will not maximize organizational value and will risk ultimate failure.

Level 4: Results

Level 4 holds the distinction of being the most misunderstood of the four levels. It is the degree to which targeted outcomes occur as a result of the learning event(s) and subsequent reinforcement.

Level 1   Level 2   Level 3   **Level 4**
Reaction   Learning   Behavior   **Results**

Level 4: Results
The degree to which targeted outcomes occur as a result of the learning event(s) and subsequent reinforcement

A common misapplication occurs when professionals or functional departments define results in terms of their small, individual area of the organization instead of globally for the entire company. This creates silos and fiefdoms that are counterproductive to organizational effectiveness. The resulting misalignment causes layers upon layers of dysfunction and waste.

Clarity regarding the true Level 4 result of an organization is critical. By definition, it is some combination of the organizational purpose and mission. In a for-profit company, it means profitably delivering the product or service to the marketplace. In a not-for-profit, government or military organization, it means accomplishing the mission.

Every organization has just one Level 4 Result. A good test of whether or not the correct Level 4 Result has been identified is a positive answer to the question, "Is this what the organization exists to do / deliver / contribute?"

While this definition of results is straightforward, frustration with the seeming inability to relate a single training class to a high-level organizational mission is common. Business results are broad and long term. They are created through the culmination of countless efforts of people, departments and environmental factors. They can take months or years to manifest.

Examples from the Story

The Premier Resort made all employees aware from their first day of the Level 4 Result at the resort:

"Every job at the resort is of equal importance in meeting our highest goal, which is the sustained profitability of the resort," Mr. Safrina continued.

Leading Indicators

Leading indicators help to bridge the gap between individual initiatives and efforts and organizational results. They are defined as short-term observations and measurements that suggest that critical behaviors are on track to create a positive impact on the desired results.

Organizations will have a number of leading indicators that encompass departmental and individual goals, each contributing to the accomplishment of the highest level results.

Leading Indicators
Short-term observations and measurements that suggest that critical behaviors are on track to create a positive impact on desired results

Common leading indicators include:

- Customer satisfaction
- Employee engagement
- Sales volume
- Cost containment
- Quality
- Market share

While leading indicators are important measurements, they must be balanced with a focus on the highest level result. For example, a company with excellent customer satisfaction scores could go out of business if it does not maintain profitability, comply with laws and regulations and keep its employees reasonably happy.

Note that customer satisfaction is an example of a goal that does not provide an affirmative answer to the question, "Is this what the organization exists to contribute?" No organization exists simply to deliver customer service alone.

Examples from the Story

The Premier Resort made each employee aware of the leading indicators for the company during orientation:

"We track three key areas at the Premier Resort: team performance, guest experience and overall resort performance.

> *You will see updated statistics each week on a poster like this in the employee break area." Mr. Safrina held up an example.*

Level 4 Summary

Every organization has just one Level 4 Result but multiple leading indicators.

Clarity surrounding the true highest result and key leading indicators is critical for organizational alignment. This organizes the efforts of all employees and departments towards the single highest goal and provides individualized feedback and encouragement to all along the way.

Relating Level 3 Behaviors to the corresponding leading indicators shows each employee how they contribute to the organization in their own way, in concert with other employees and departments.

Chapter 13
The Kirkpatrick
Foundational Principles

THE KIRKPATRICK FOUNDATIONAL Principles
were developed in 2009, the 50th anniversary of the
publishing of the works that have become known as
the Kirkpatrick Model.

Because the Kirkpatrick Model had developed
organically over the prior 50 years, there were cases
of misuse and misinterpretation. The intent of
the principles is to illustrate the meaning that Dr.
Kirkpatrick, Sr., intended when he published his first
works.

This chapter outlines the Kirkpatrick Foundational
Principles and provides examples of them from the
story.

Kirkpatrick Foundational Principles
1. The end is the beginning
2. Return on expectations (ROE) is the ultimate indicator of value
3. Business partnership is necessary to bring about positive ROE
4. Value must be created before it can be demonstrated
5. A compelling chain of evidence demonstrates your bottom-line value

Kirkpatrick Foundational Principle #1

The end is the beginning.

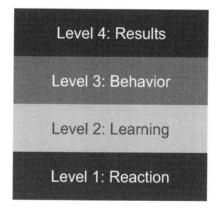

Effective training and development begins before the program even starts. Don Kirkpatrick says it best on page 26 of Evaluating Training Programs: The Four Levels (1st Edition, Berrett-Koehler, 1993):

"Trainers must begin, with desired results (Level 4) and then determine what behavior (Level 3) is needed to accomplish them. Then trainers must determine the attitudes, knowledge, and skills (Level 2) that are necessary to bring about the desired behavior(s). The final challenge is to present the training program in a way that enables the participants not only to learn what they need to know but also to react favorably to the program (Level 1)."

It is important that the results are at the organizational level and are defined in measurable terms so that all involved can see the ultimate destination of the initiative. Clearly-defined results will increase the likelihood that resources will be most effectively and efficiently used to accomplish the mission.

Attempting to apply the four levels after an initiative has been developed and delivered makes it difficult, if not impossible, to create significant training value. All four levels must be considered at every step in the program's design, execution and measurement.

Kirkpatrick Foundational Principle #2

Return on expectations (ROE) is the ultimate indicator of value.

When executives ask for new training, many learning professionals retreat to their departments and begin designing and developing suitable programs. While a cursory needs assessment may be conducted, it is rarely taken to the extent to which expectations of the training's contribution to Level 4 Results are completely clear.

> **Return on Expectations**
> What a successful training initiative delivers to key business stakeholders demonstrating the degree to which their expectations have been satisfied

Stakeholder expectations define the value that training professionals are responsible for delivering. Learning professionals must ask the stakeholders questions to clarify and refine their expectations on all four Kirkpatrick levels, from leading indicators to the Level 4 Result.

Determining the leading indicators upon which the success of an initiative will be measured is a negotiation process in which the training professional ensures that the expectations are satisfying to the stakeholder and realistic to achieve with the resources available.

Once stakeholder expectations are clear, learning professionals then need to convert those typically general wants into observable, measurable leading indicators by asking the question, "What will success look like to you?" It may take a series of questions to arrive at the final indicators of program success.

Agreement surrounding leading indicators at the

beginning of a project eliminates the need to later attempt to prove the value of the initiative. It is understood from the beginning that if the leading indicator targets are met, the initiative will be viewed as a success.

Kirkpatrick Foundational Principle #3

Business partnership is necessary to bring about positive ROE.

As noted previously, training events in and of themselves typically produce about 15% on-the-job application. To increase application and therefore program results, additional actions must be taken before and after formal training.

Historically, the role of learning professionals has been to accomplish Levels 1 and 2, or just to complete the training event alone. Not surprisingly, this is where learning professionals spend most of their time.

Producing ROE, however, requires a strong Level 3 execution plan. Therefore, it is critical not only to call upon business partners to help identify what success will look like, but also to design a cooperative effort throughout the learning and performance processes in order to maximize results.

Before training, learning professionals need to partner with supervisors and managers to prepare participants for training. Even more critical is the role of the supervisor or manager after the training. They are the key people who reinforce newly-learned knowledge and skills through support and accountability. <u>The degree to which this reinforcement and coaching occurs directly correlates to improved performance and positive outcomes.</u>

Kirkpatrick Foundational Principle #4

Value must be created before it can be demonstrated.

Up to 90% of training resources are spent on the design, development and delivery of training events that yield the previously-mentioned 15% on-the-job application. Reinforcement that occurs after the training event produces the highest level of learning effectiveness, followed by activities that occur before the learning event, yet each typically garners only 5% of the training time and budget.

Currently, learning professionals are putting most of their resources into the part of the training process that produces the lowest level of business or organizational results. They are spending relatively little time in the pre-training and follow-up activities that translate into the positive behavior change and subsequent results (Levels 3 and 4) that organizations seek.

Formal training is the foundation of performance and results. To create ultimate value and ROE, however, strong attention must be given to Level 3 activities.

To create maximum value within their organizations, learning professionals must redefine their roles and extend their expertise, involvement and influence into Levels 3 and 4.

Kirkpatrick Foundational Principle #5

A compelling chain of evidence demonstrates your bottom-line value.

Level 1   Level 2   Level 3   Level 4

Chain of Evidence
Data, information and testimonies at each of the four levels that, when presented in sequence, act to demonstrate the value obtained from a business partnership initiative.

The training industry is on trial, accused by business leaders of consuming resources in excess of the value delivered to the organization.

Following the Kirkpatrick Foundational Principles and using the Kirkpatrick Model will create a chain of evidence that demonstrates the organizational value of the entire business partnership effort. It consists of quantitative and qualitative data that sequentially connect the four levels and show the ultimate contribution of learning and reinforcement to the organization.

When workplace learning professionals work in concert with their key business partners, this chain of evidence supports the partnership effort and demonstrates the organizational value of working as a team to accomplish the overall mission.

The chain of evidence serves to unify the learning and business functions, not to isolate training or set it apart. This unity is critical for Level 3 execution, where organizational value is produced.

When presenting a chain of evidence, keep in mind what is most important to the stakeholder audience. Generally speaking, data at Levels 3 and 4 are of most interest. Data related to Levels 1 and 2 should be limited unless a detailed report is requested specifically.

Part III:
Getting Started

"Be the change you wish
to see in the world."

Mahatma Gandhi

AT THIS POINT, you have heard the inspiring story of Chai and learned about the methodology that helped him to excel in his role at the Premier Resort.

We hope you are energized and ready to create the same passion within your own organization. While executing business partnership takes strong senior leadership and potentially years of effort, each and every person in an organization can take small steps on their own. Many small steps can create great strides and significant improvements.

If you're with us, here are some steps for getting started.

THE KIRKPATRICK BUSINESS Partnership Model is a holistic model within which business units and training work together to accomplish organizational goals. It is simplified with the acronym PARTNER.

Follow these steps to begin to create the kind of alignment, performance and organizational success enjoyed by the Premier Resort.

Kirkpatrick Business Partnership Steps

Pledge to work together

Address jury issues

Refine expectations to define outcomes

Target critical behaviors and required drivers

Necessities for success

Execute the initiative

ROE Retun on expectations

Pledge to work together

Business partnership starts with a request for training to help with a business problem. Unfortunately, this request rarely comes in a clear message like, "We want to decrease turnover by 5% this fiscal year." Instead, you are more likely to hear, "We need leadership training for our managers. We have one hour in the next committee meeting. Have something ready." While these requests are often delivered as a "training order," like a meal at a fast food restaurant, it is preferable to getting no "orders" at all.

Pledging to work together actually begins before the request for help. It starts with building a relationship of listening to and understanding the overall needs and direction of the business and earning trust from business executives to elicit a request for assistance. This pre-step may require training professionals to uncover the biggest needs, problems and business opportunities in the organization.

It also involves training professionals embracing the role of supporting key organizational initiatives by increasing benefits (revenue, profits, market share) or diminishing liabilities (accidents, lawsuits, scrap). There is no such thing as a "training initiative" in business partnership. Instead, training and reinforcement are conducted in support of key business initiatives.

Through discussion, training and business leaders should come to an agreement that a cross-functional team will help everyone to accomplish their goals and that they want to be on that team.

Address jury issues

Training professionals should realize and accept that their performance will be judged by the business or organizational leaders. These people can be considered their "jury," sitting in judgment of the value they bring to the organization.

First, identify who sits on the jury. Whether in a large corporation, government agency, small family business, or contractor situation, every training professional has a jury. The jury changes depending on the particular initiative at hand.

Second, ask the jury what they expect the training portion of the initiative to deliver. This typically requires a two-way conversation. Initial expectations often need to be restated in terms that can be delivered with training, which is by definition something requiring knowledge, skill, or a certain attitude. Reinforcement and follow-up after training must be considered as well. And of course, the jury must feel that the efforts discussed will meet their business needs.

Third, the type and format of evidence proving that business needs have been met should be discussed and agreed upon before moving forward. For example, the CFO likely wishes to see different evidence than the marketing manager.

Refine expectations to define outcomes

With jury expectations clarified, the next step is to convert the expectations into targeted, observable, measurable Level 4 outcomes. This is a component of the process that many professionals believe they perform, but few actually accomplish.

Training professionals should have their consulting hats on when they meet with the jury. Be prepared with a few realistic outcomes for the requested training program that could be delivered successfully within the described parameters and could satisfy business partner expectations.

Remember: The end is the beginning. All efforts should be focused on achieving organizational objectives. If the proposed efforts do not clearly support the desired outcomes, the purpose behind the expenditure of resources should be questioned.

Targeted outcomes are observable and measurable indicators of organizational success. It typically takes some discussion to identify the measurable indicators for a given program. For example, management may express an expectation of greater safety on the job. The corresponding targeted outcome would be a reduction in the number of lost-time injuries on the job, which contributes to overall profitability and company image.

Target critical behaviors and required drivers

Once the targeted outcomes are identified, training and key managers or supervisors will work together to identify two key factors: critical behaviors and required drivers. This step often is overlooked, and well-meaning training professionals attempt to build training programs based on high-level outcomes with no information as to what is or is not happening on the job currently.

Critical behaviors and required drivers are the keys to the successful implementation (Level 3) and ultimate accomplishment of targeted outcomes. This step is critical to designing and conducting an initiative that pays dividends for the time and resources invested in it.

Critical behaviors refer to the most important actions that training graduates must consistently engage in on the job to create the desired results. They also must be defined in observable, measurable terms. For example, after training, accountants will follow document standards for all reports.

Required drivers are the tools incorporated into the training and follow-up that encourage the desired new behaviors, monitor their execution, and reinforce and reward their successful adoption on the job.

The responsibility for drivers is shared by training, support and management staff, and other support functions like Human Resources, Information Systems and Accounting. Creating a strong required drivers plan at the beginning of an initiative and obtaining buy-in for the resources and efforts required is critical to a successful initiative.

Required drivers act as an early warning detection system to flag substandard performance. The cause can be analyzed and remedied so the initiative stays on track to accomplish targeted results.

Necessities for success

Outside of a laboratory environment, there is no way to isolate an initiative and its impact from other organizational effects. Every company has variables that could negatively affect targeted outcomes for an initiative if not addressed. Addressing these types of issues and creating the best possible environment for the initiative to succeed is what is referred to as necessities for success.

Examples of necessities for success include preparing managers for a culture of coaching that will leverage and reinforce newly-learned skills, setting up software programs to streamline new processes, and communicating reporting and accountability structures. While required drivers are ongoing support processes and systems, necessities for success are more often events or projects.

> **Necessities for success**
>
> Prerequisite items, events, or conditions that set the stage for success and that help avoid problems before they get a chance to reduce the impact of the training initiative

Execute the initiative

This step includes designing, developing and delivering the training content, as well as initiating the drivers and measurements that will occur after training. This step is fairly familiar for most training professionals, with two exceptions. First, there is a greater focus on what happens after training than on the training program itself. Second, measurement and evaluation tools are built alongside the training and reinforcement content.

This step is straightforward in the Kirkpatrick Business Partnership Model because of the work that has been accomplished in prior steps. This allows more time to be spent supporting critical behaviors and required drivers after training.

Progress should be tracked and reported throughout the initiative so that stakeholders remain apprised of the program status. The reporting system should be designed and built and roles assigned during this stage as well.

ROE - Return on expectations

Return on expectations means taking the data collected throughout the initiative at each of the four Kirkpatrick levels, creating a logical chain of evidence and presenting it to the jury in a compelling manner.

If training professionals want business leaders to regard them as true business partners, this step is essential. Jury members are required to collect this type of data for all of their own initiatives to obtain approval for their departmental budgets. As a valued business partner, part of training is walking in those shoes by gathering data and presenting it professionally in the same way. This is critical to gaining respect and trust.

This step, like the previous one, is fairly straightforward if the beginning of the process is completed properly. It is simply a matter of putting together the requested evidence into a polished presentation and practicing the delivery with a mock audience until it feels comfortable.

Chapter 15
Building Business
Partnership

THIS CHAPTER PROVIDES specific actions that an individual can take to begin to build business partnership within their own organization.

Find an executive sponsor

Even the most enthusiastic associate needs a champion if the culture of an organization requires some modification. Share this book with a high-level manager or executive who you think will see the vision. Then schedule a brief discussion to talk about how the story applies to your organization.

Create a cross-functional council

Work with your executive sponsor to create a cross-functional council to discuss and implement business partnership in your organization. Ideally, your executive sponsor will agree to chair the committee.

Complete the business partnership inventory

To give you an idea of where your organization stands, have each member of the newly-formed council complete the business partnership inventory at the end of this chapter.

Discuss business partnership inventory results

At the first council meeting, discuss each person's inventory results.

- In what areas is your organization doing well?
- Which areas could be improved?
- Which areas might be good places to start with "quick wins"?
- Which areas should be the collective focus, with the greatest chance to move the organization forward?

Identify the organization's highest goal

What is the highest goal of the organization? What are the leading indicators or other measures that the company holds important?

Example

King Enterprises is a supplier of industrial parts used in assembly lines. Their goal is profitable sales growth.

Leading indicators that they are on track for profitable growth include:

- Sales to existing customers
- New customer acquisition
- Customer service ratings
- Customer retention
- Employee satisfaction
- Employee retention

If you are reading this and thinking, "If I had the power to create a committee, we would already have these ideas in place," fair enough. We encourage you to complete the business partnership inventory on the following pages on your own, and think about how you can follow the preceding steps in your own position or department.

We also encourage you to reach out and find other like-minded professionals in your organization. What starts with one person can become a powerful movement that can change your entire organization for the better.

Kirkpatrick Business Partnership Inventory

Instructions: Objectively rate, on a scale of 1 to 3, the degree to which each statement describes your organization.

1 = Low
This statement seldom describes us

2 = Medium
This statement describes us some of the time

3 = High
This statement describes us most or all of the time

_____ 1. Our learning and business functions work together to respond to problems, needs or opportunities.

_____ 2. We have a good process for determining whether training requests are truly issues that can be resolved with training.

_____ 3. Our program development processes align well to business needs.

_____ 4. When conducting a needs assessment, our process includes identifying "what success will look like" for major initiatives.

_____ 5. We engage subject matter experts in the design and development of our training programs.

_____ 6. Prior to training, line managers/supervisors sit with participants and share expectations for training and subsequent on-the-job application.

_____ 7. We use business leaders in the delivery of key training programs.

_____ 8. We establish specific job competencies and weave them into training.

_____ 9. We align our competencies to on-the-job behavioral application.

_____ 10. We effectively evaluate Level 1 Reaction for our training programs.

_____ 11. We effectively evaluate Level 2 Learning for our training programs.

_____ 12. We effectively evaluate Level 3 Behavior for our training programs.

_____ 13. We effectively evaluate Level 4 Results for major programs and initiatives.

_____ 14. We have conducted effective (training) impact studies in order to demonstrate the value of learning to the business.

_____ 15. Business managers and supervisors provide feedback and coaching to their direct reports to maximize the impact of training.

_____ 16. We determine and monitor key drivers that will encourage or discourage the transfer of learning to behavior.

_____ 17. We develop effective job aids for both participants and managers to help them to apply what is learned in training.

_____ 18. We effectively utilize technology to streamline training and evaluation.

_____ 19. We effectively demonstrate the value of learning to the bottom line.

_____ 20. Overall, I believe our organization has a learning and performance culture.

Now, total up the points for each item and compare your score to the rating scale:

Total Score: _____

60 – 50	Excellent
49 – 42	Very good
41 – 34	Good
33 – 26	Fair
25 – 20	Poor

This score indicates how well your organization is leveraging learning and development to support highest level business results.

Chapter 16
Call to Action

THIS IS YOUR chance to become a Brunei
Window Washer or to develop a team of like-minded
professionals.

Take a moment below to document a few specific
actions you can take in your own role to enhance the
level of business partnership in your organization:

_____

_____

_____

_____

_____

_____

Surround yourself with like-minded people in your organization (or community), and form a committee dedicated to building business partnership. List potential partners and related notes:

_____

_____

_____

_____

_____

❧ ❧

Visit the Brunei Window Washer webpage for more specific ideas about how you can get started and additional resources:

Brunei Window Washer Webpage

http://bit.ly/BruneiWindowWasher

We wish you the best of success in creating a meaningful purpose in your own career and those of others. We love to hear from people like you, so please drop us an email and let us know how it's going!

J D Kirkpatrick, PhD   *Wendy Kayser Kirkpatrick*

Jim and Wendy Kirkpatrick
information@kirkpatrickpartners.com

Afterword

Greetings Readers,

When I developed the four levels over five decades ago, I honestly had no idea where it would all go. I am so pleased that they have come far since then. I am officially retired, but that doesn't mean that I have lost interest in where the Kirkpatrick Model is headed.

Over the past several years, I have proudly watched Jim, my son, and Wendy, my daughter-in-law, along with global ambassadors of the New World Kirkpatrick Model, take the four levels to new heights. New applications of the model have occurred in enterprise evaluation, key policies and procedures, and individual goal achievement. Powerful enhancements have been made to each of the levels, as well as the connection of Levels 2 and 3.

Jim and Wendy have written this book to highlight additional new directions. This book is nothing like the others we have written. It was written in such a way to highlight a principle that I have lived by and taught for years. I call it "PIE;" the "P" stands for "practical," the "I" for "interactive," and the "E" for "enjoyable." While this book is strongly practical, it really hits on the "enjoyable" aspect of PIE, showing us that evaluation does not have to be stuffy and academic.

There is something else about this book that is

particularly important. It brings the entire Kirkpatrick Model, especially the elusive Levels 3 and 4, to the individual level. This is truly cutting edge. Individuals need to be clear about what is expected of them, inspired in their work and able to see the contribution they are making to the whole. It is the individual, when all is said and done, that drives cultural change.

Some have asked me, "Don, are you pleased about the new directions Jim and Wendy are taking the four levels?" Well, let me save you having to ask. The answer is a resounding, "yes." Any way the four levels can be applied that will help more people in more powerful ways, I am all for it!

Learn, enjoy and apply!

Don Kirkpatrick

References

American Society for Training and Development. (2006). *State of the Industry Report*. Alexandria, VA: Author.

American Society for Training and Development. (2009). *The Value of Evaluation: Making Training Evaluations More Effective*. Alexandria, VA: Author.

Brinkerhoff, R.O. (2006). *Telling Training's Story: Evaluation Made Simple, Credible, and Effective*. San Francisco, CA: Berrett-Koehler Publishers.

Kirkpatrick, D.L. (2010) *Evaluating Human Relations Programs for Industrial Foremen and Supervisors*. St. Louis, MO: Kirkpatrick Publishing.

Kirkpatrick, D.L., & Kirkpatrick, J.D. (2005). *Transferring Learning to Behavior*. San Francisco, CA: Berrett-Koehler Publishers.

Kirkpatrick, D.L., & Kirkpatrick, J.D. (2006). *Evaluating Training Programs: The Four Levels* (3rd ed.). San Francisco, CA: Berrett-Koehler Publishers.

Kirkpatrick, J.D., & Kirkpatrick, W.K. (2009). *Kirkpatrick Then and Now*. St. Louis, MO: Kirkpatrick Publishing.

Kirkpatrick, J.D., & Kirkpatrick, W.K. (2010). *Training on Trial*. New York, NY: AMACOM.

About the Authors

James D. (Jim) Kirkpatrick, PhD, is a senior consultant for Kirkpatrick Partners. His major area of expertise is the Kirkpatrick Business Partnership Model.

Jim consults for Fortune 500 companies around the world, including Harley-Davidson, Booz Allen Hamilton, L'Oreal, Clarian, Ingersoll Rand, Honda, the Royal Air Force and GE Healthcare.

Jim is the oldest son of Dr. Don Kirkpatrick, the creator of the Kirkpatrick Model.

Wendy Kayser Kirkpatrick is the president of Kirkpatrick Partners. She is a certified instructional designer.

Wendy draws on two decades of experience in training, retailing and marketing to make her programs relevant and impactful with measurable results.

Jim and Wendy are proud to have the privilege of carrying on the landmark work of Don Kirkpatrick through their company, Kirkpatrick Partners. They attribute their success to the strong network of Kirkpatrick Community members around the world, who regularly apply the model and inspire them with stories of success.

About Kirkpatrick Partners

Kirkpatrick Partners transforms training professionals and learning functions into true strategic business partners. They equip people to create significant value for their business stakeholders and demonstrate impact to the bottom line.

Through expertise and experience, Kirkpatrick Partners teaches the science of the Kirkpatrick Model in order to successfully facilitate the execution of business strategy. Equally importantly, they approach their work with the heart to improve lives and change corporate cultures.

Please join the Kirkpatrick Community of learning professionals that is working to make a real difference. Consider becoming Kirkpatrick Certified.

Many companies base their work on the Kirkpatrick Model. Why not work with The One and Only Kirkpatrick® company and experience authentic Kirkpatrick products and services? Your business deserves the original and best program evaluation methodology.

Kirkpatrick Partners is here to help you on your journey to professional fulfillment and mission accomplishment. If you have a story, challenge, success or anything you would like to share, please contact the authors at: information@kirkpatrickpartners.com.

With your permission, your stories and experiences could be published in future works.

Visit *http://bit.ly/BruneiWindowWasher* for more information.

Visit Kirkpatrickpartners.com

- Register to receive FREE weekly articles and tips

- Use the FREE online resources library, containing over 60 articles, recordings and tools

- Access the calendar of upcoming appearances and events

- Find out more about scheduling a customized training session for your team

Read All the
Kirkpatrick Books

Training on Trial

"*Training on Trial* should be a required read for anyone in the business of buying, building, and delivering training."

Judith Hale, Ph.D., CPT
Hale Associates

Kirkpatrick Then and Now: A Strong Foundation for the Future

"Kirkpatrick's four levels is the best I've ever seen in evaluating training effectiveness. It is sequentially integrated and comprehensive. It goes far beyond 'smile sheets' into actual learning, behavior changes and actual results, including long-term evaluation. An outstanding model!"

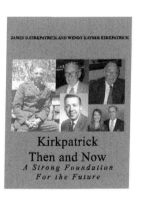

Stephen R. Covey,
Author of *The 7 Habits of
Highly Effective People*

Implementing the Four Levels

"As no industry dynamics are exactly the same, I found the flexibility of the options/tools/ resources around learning evaluations to be credible and comprehensive."

Barbara Hewitt
Executive Director
MGM Grand University

Transferring Learning to Behavior

"A must-read for every trainer and performance consultant.

Chock-full of real-life cases and implement-now ideas, Don and Jim have revisited the basics with a new twist – one you won't want to miss!"

Elaine Biech
Author of *Business of Consulting and Training for Dummies*

Evaluating Training Programs: The Four Levels, 3rd Edition

"Don Kirkpatrick's name has long been synonymous with evaluation. This book provides, in one place, Don's best thinking on the subject.

I highly recommend it!"

Bob Pike, President
Creative Training Techniques
International, Inc.

Made in the USA
Charleston, SC
02 November 2014